This book belongs to
YOU
dear

The River in the Sky

Curious Bea learns about Oxygen

For Mia

CORNEST
Publications

This is Bea! She's only five
but can absolutely drive
her mum, a lawyer,
both her brothers
and her astronaut dad
positively MAD!

... with questions that come out of nowhere and from ... everywhere!!

2

Perhaps it's true, dear ________
She's just like YOU!!

'Why are you wearing that?'
In her Dad's lap Bea sat,
all wrapped in his hug so cosy
with her blue baby blanky.
This was when
they were in his den.

'It's a space helmet,' said Dad.
Bea wrote this on a notepad.

'It's to breathe with,' he explained.
Bea's head titled; her neck craned.
'Why don't you need one down
here on earth?'   Bea frowned.

Bea loved to question.
Every day was a learning
session!
Perhaps it's true, dear
that she's just like YOU!!

Out they went to the garden,
the sun was all shiny and golden.
Why is the sky so blue?
Bea wished she knew.

Isn't it true, Dear
She's just like you?

Bea's dad said, taking her hand,
'There's a thin blue band
that hugs our planet.'
'Auwē!' said Bea, 'like my
blanket?'

'Yes! Our planet's so special,
we're in our own little bubble.'
'What's it called, you think?'
Bea asked with a blink.

Bea loved to question ...
Do you have that
in common
with her, dear reader?
Are you always eager
for answers that surprise?
Oh! You'll soon be so wise!

'The atmosphere ...
that's what it's called, dear.
That's what the earth is covered by.'

Bea thought, My oh my!
 It was the biggest word
she'd ever heard!

So the earth has a helmet of its own!
Bea's mind was totally blown!
She was in a proper state
and Dad said, 'Isn't that great?'

Other than asking
Bea loved learning.
Perhaps it's true dear
____

that's just like ...
YOU!! .

They had pizza for tea,
the whole Kiwi family
... (so yum!)

Hua, Tyan, Dad and Mum
and Bea – we mustn't forget!
This was at sunset.

So, in five they sliced the large pizza.
No one got extra.
Equal pieces, they'd decided,
'cause they were all so fair-minded.

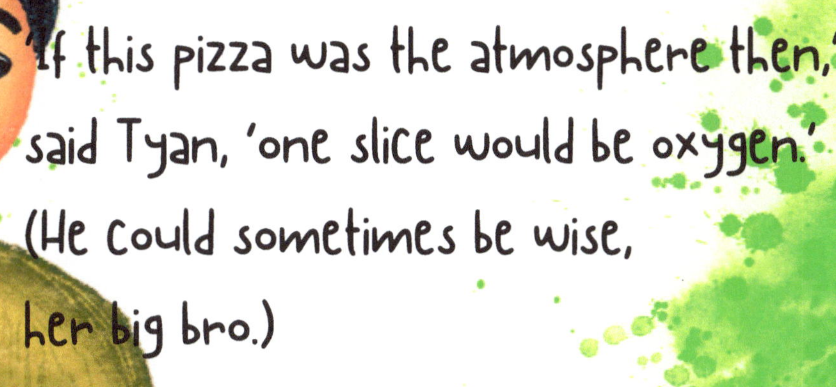

'If this pizza was the atmosphere then,'
said Tyan, 'one slice would be oxygen.'
(He could sometimes be wise,
her big bro.)

Bea leaned forward
and said, 'Oh?'

It was time for
a question or two
I'm sure that's no surprise
to you!
'Cause Bea's just like you dear
and that's so true!

'Oxygen? What's that?'
asked Bea out pat—
she wasn't a fraidy cat.
Mum said, 'It's in the air . . .
it's everywhere!'

'But I can't see it!'
Bea was desperate
to find out
what this was all about.

Isn't it true, dear ________
She's just like YOU?

'Remember when we built a fire at camp?' asked Dad.

'Yes! It made me perspire so bad!'

'And I blew on the flames to make them leap?'

'Auwē!, it grew to be one big burning heap!'

'Twas the oxygen in my breath that fed the flames.'

How curious! 'Oh?' Bea exclaimed.

She was thinking, you see —
How could that be?
  Her dad looked at her. He knew her too well.
    She still had a ton of questions, he could tell.
So, he said, 'If we had too much oxygen,
we would all fry!'
Bea thought, What? How? Why?
'What if we had too little?'
  asked Bea, all a-fiddle.

She could always find
a reason
to ask another question.
Isn't it true, dear
she's just like ... YOU?

'That's simple,' said Dad with a sigh.
'We would all die!'
He added, 'So we need just enough
of that life-giving stuff ...'

'Of oxygen,' interrupted Tyan.
(He loved to do that —
to interrupt a chat!

Bea would not be left behind.
She said, 'Tyan, do you mind?'
and added, 'Out of five parts of
atmosphere, oxygen should be a mere – '
'One!' said Tyan, interrupting again!

But there was no doubt
Bea'd already worked that out!
And now she wanted to know,
'From where does it flow?'

Isn't it true,
dear ________
that you wished YOU
knew, too?

'Special creatures in the oceans ... in their millions
make our oxygen,' said Mum.

Millions is a big sum!

'What are they called?'
asked Bea, enthralled.

'They're called diatoms,' Mum said.
Bea asked, 'Oh, how are they fed?'
Her head bustled with questions, as
this info had turned her into a spazz!

'On bits of
stones and rock,'
said Tyan with flair.

'Auwē!' said Bea,
and then ...
'From where?'

'There's a river, up high.'
said Hua, 'up in the sky.'
'Are you being silly?' Bea asked hotly.
(Sometimes Hua could be a bully!)
'No,' said Dad,
'he's right, honey.'

Well, dear ________________
if you took a trip in a magnificent,
ginormous spaceship
(Surely someday you might
just take that flight …),
you would see the river
in the sky, above Amazonia,
the rainforest, up high!
Wouldn't YOU like to spy,
this crazy river
that can fly?
44

Other books in the Chemist Bea series:

Born in the Heart of a Star

(Bea learns about Carbon)

The Ha Ha Gas

(Bea learns about Nitrogen)

Find them online at major bookstores or contact the publishers at: cornestpublications@gmail.com